THE DOG
Artlist Collection

This book is officially licensed by Winning Moves UK Ltd, owners of the Top Trumps registered trademark.

THE DOG brand © 2007 artlist INTERNATIONAL.
Licensed by 4Kids Entertainment.

Carolyn Menteith has asserted her right to be identified as the author of this book.

British Library Cataloguing-in-Publication Data:
A catalogue record for this book is available from the British Library

ISBN 978 1 84425 432 3

Library of Congress catalog card no. 2007922002

Published by Haynes Publishing,
Sparkford, Yeovil, Somerset BA22 7JJ, UK
Tel: +44 (0)1963 442030 Fax: +44 (0)1963 440001
Email: sales@haynes.co.uk
Website: www.haynes.co.uk

Haynes North America, Inc., 861 Lawrence Drive,
Newbury Park California 91320, USA

Printed and bound in Great Britain by J. H. Haynes & Co. Ltd, Sparkford

All photographs copyright artlist INTERNATIONAL with the following exceptions: Border Terrier, Cairn Terrier, Great Dane, Pointer, Rhodesian Ridgeback, Springer Spaniel and Staffordshire Bull Terrier, all of which are copyright Eaglemoss Publications/Simon Anning, from The Dog Collection (www.the-dog-collection.co.uk).

The Author

Carolyn Menteith is a dog trainer and behaviourist with over 20 years' experience of working with animals. As well as writing for national magazines and featuring on radio as a dog expert, she has presented TV programmes such as *What's Up Dog* (Carlton), *Celebrity Dog School* (BBC1 for Children in Need), *Barking Babes* (Granada) and *Top Dog* (Animal Planet).

TOP TRUMPS®

THE DOG

Artlist Collection

CONTENTS

HOUSE

CONTENTS

HOUSE

About
Top Trumps

It's now more than 30 years since Britain's kids first caught the Top Trumps craze. The game remained hugely popular until the 1990s, when it slowly drifted into obscurity. Then, in 1999, UK games company Winning Moves discovered it, bought it, dusted it down, gave it a thorough makeover and introduced it to a whole new generation. And so the Top Trumps legend continues.

Nowadays, there are Top Trumps titles for just about everyone, with subjects about animals, cars, ships, aircraft and all the great films and TV shows. Top Trumps is now even more popular than before. In Britain, a pack of Top Trumps is bought every six seconds! And it's not just British children who love the game. Children in Australasia, the Far East, the Middle East, all over Europe and in North America can buy Top Trumps at their local shops.

Today you can even play the game on the internet, interactive DVD, your games console and even your mobile phone.

HOUSE   **You've played the game...**

Now read the book!

Haynes Publishing and Top Trumps have teamed up to bring you this exciting new Top Trumps book, in which you will find even more pictures, facts and ratings.

Top Trumps: The Dog features 80 breeds from around the world, from the smallest to the largest, the laziest to the most energetic. Packed with fascinating facts, photographs from The Dog Artlist Collection and ratings to allow comparison between breeds, this is the essential pocket guide. We've also included a short introduction to each of the seven dog groups and some useful Top 5 lists.

Look out for other Top Trumps books from Haynes Publishing – even more facts, even more fun!

THE GROUPS

As anyone who has ever watched Crufts on the TV will know, every breed of dog falls into a different 'group' depending on their original job description or, in other words, what they were originally bred to do. These groups are Working, Pastoral, Gundog, Hound, Terrier, Toy and Utility. Anyone searching for their perfect dog should start by looking at the breeds in these groups to find what characteristics describe their ideal companion.

HOUSE

Working dogs

The dogs in this group were bred to do very specific and demanding jobs. The guarding breeds are included in this group, as are sledge dogs, search and rescue dogs, some hunting and fighting dogs, and even dogs to help fishermen. These are mostly large and powerful dogs who need experienced, active owners with an interest in training and socialising – and with a large house and garden. They are mostly not dogs for first-time owners and often aren't ideal family pets. They need dog-owning experts to give them the lifestyle they need so they can become the fabulous dogs they are designed to be.

Pastoral Dogs

This group was bred to work with sheep, cattle and other cloven footed animals – even including reindeer! They are great for active, experienced owners, or families who want to do a lot of training and canine activities, who have a good-sized house and garden and who, in some cases, enjoy a lot of grooming! These dogs are designed to work all day every day and so are not dogs for couch potatoes! If you choose to own one of these breeds, you need to be able to provide plenty of exercise and stimulation to keep them healthy and happy. These are dogs who need a job to do and an owner who is going to provide them with an outlet for their boundless energy. They are among the brightest of the dogs, and so are easily trained, but because they are so clever they are far more likely to get into all kinds of trouble if they don't have guidance, or if they are bored.

Gundogs

This group was originally bred to find live game or else to retrieve game that had been shot by hunters. They are generally ideal for first-time dog owners, couples and families – as long as they are active! Ideally, they need a good-sized house and garden. These are happy, fun, often boisterous dogs who make great companions and are excellent all-round family dogs, with a size to suit everyone. They are intelligent, easy to train and can generally learn to get on with all family members – even the cat! Sadly their reputation as excellent family dogs has led to them being owned by people who don't realise that they are bred to work and so need a lot of exercise to keep them happy and healthy – and slimline!

Hounds

The dogs in this group were originally bred for hunting. They vary in size and shape more than any other group, with the smallest being the Miniature Dachshund starting at a tiny 13cm, while the tallest is the giant of the dog world, the Irish Wolfhound, who can reach an amazing 90cm! They split into two groups: sight hounds and scent hounds depending on whether they use their eyes or nose to hunt. Mostly these are fairly laid-back and dignified dogs to live with, although some can be rather aloof (especially the sight hounds). These dogs need a lot of exercise and enjoy nothing more than long walks in the great outdoors However, the thrill of the chase (or the scent) is so strong in this group that they can be very challenging to train to come back when called! Many of the breeds in this group are not reliable with other animals, and while many can, with extreme care, learn to live with their own cats, they may never be safe with strange ones. Hounds are ideal for all dog owners who are prepared to securely fence their garden, do a lot of work on recall and/or not let them off the lead. They also need a good-sized house and a large garden to run in, as they do need free-running exercise.

Terriers

These dogs were bred for hunting vermin, and so were selected to be brave and tough so they could pursue rats and other animals, often far bigger than themselves, both above and below ground. As these dogs were frequently required to vanish into the holes and burrows of their quarry, they are mostly small dogs, although there are some exceptions such as the Airedale, who can be up to 61cm high! While these dogs are small, they should not be mistaken for lapdogs; they are just as feisty as their ancestors! As a result, they may not have a lot of patience with children unless they are well trained (both the dogs AND the children!) and because of their original job they may not be good with cats or other small animals. If you want a small dog with lots of character and personality (and don't mind a bit of noise!), and you enjoy lots of exercise then a terrier could be your perfect dog.

Toy

These dogs have been purpose-bred to be companions to humans. They have friendly personalities and love attention. Many from this group make ideal first time dogs. However, some are so small that they can be too delicate for boisterous family life. They can live easily in smaller properties and in towns or cities, and need less exercise than the other groups, but still should be walked every day. Despite their size, they are intelligent companions who are easy to train but they must be treated like a dog. Far too many become spoilt, pampered lap dogs who are carried everywhere and never have a true 'doggie life'. These then often become overly protective of their owners and also become impossible to leave alone for even the briefest of moments – which is very hard to live with. Toy dogs should be extroverted and happy companions, and so they need sensible owners who want a small dog and not a fashion accessory. They make fabulous fun pets, and many can excel in some of the canine sports such as mini-agility.

Utility

This group consists of an extremely mixed bunch of all shapes and sizes, and includes some of the oldest recorded breeds of dog. All have been selectively bred to perform a specific job not included in the other categories. In other words, these are the dogs that don't fit anywhere else! When looking at dogs from the utility group, make sure you know what their original job was, and that will largely dictate their personality and needs. Their grooming and exercise requirements will, of course, depend on their size and hairiness!

AFGHAN HOUND

Height	63–74cm
How much exercise?	🐾 🐾 🐾 🐾
How easy to train?	🐾
How noisy?	🐾
How much grooming?	🐾 🐾 🐾 🐾 🐾
How rare?	🐾 🐾 🐾 🐾 🐾

Group – Hound
Country of origin – Afghanistan
Originally bred to chase large prey

The Afghan Hound is probably the most elegant and spectacular of all the hounds, with his aristocratically long nose, curled tail and very long, flowing, fine coat. This is a dog for people who like a lot of grooming, and who appreciate a companion who is rather independent and aloof. The Afghan Hound is certainly a challenge to train, as he seems to feel it is beneath him, and he may never have a reliable recall – as the thrill of the chase is often just too strong. Despite this, he was born to run, and so owners need to have plenty of secure space to make plenty of free-running exercise possible. The Afghan Hound is a free spirit and needs an owner who appreciates that, but despite his aloofness he is affectionate to his owner, tolerates children well, isn't above playing the clown at times, and is playful with other dogs. Cats however are another matter!

HOUSE

AIREDALE TERRIER

Height	56–61cm
How much exercise?	🐾 🐾 🐾 🐾
How easy to train?	🐾 🐾 🐾
How noisy?	🐾 🐾 🐾 🐾
How much grooming?	🐾 🐾 🐾
How rare?	🐾 🐾 🐾 🐾

Group – Terrier
Country of origin – England
Originally bred to hunt and kill otters

The Airedale is by far the largest of the terriers, and so is easily recognised by his size but also by his beard and his all-weather, hard, wiry black and tan coat. This is a breed that can often be a challenge for owners – terrier attitude in such a large body can be difficult to manage! Lots of training and early socialisation are needed to make sure this breed is good with other dogs and strangers, but no amount of socialisation will make many of them good with small animals or cats! The Airedale needs lots of exercise, and, with an experienced and determined owner, he can be a wonderful companion. The Airedale is a confident, strong-minded dog who, while affectionate with his owner, still keeps an air of independence. To get the best out of this dog, owners have to earn his respect, as the Airedale likes to feel he is working 'with' his owner and not 'for' him. He will need regular grooming and stripping to keep his coat in good condition.

HOUSE

AKITA

Height	61–71cm
How much exercise?	🐾 🐾 🐾 🐾
How easy to train?	🐾 🐾 🐾 🐾
How noisy?	🐾
How much grooming?	🐾 🐾 🐾
How rare?	🐾 🐾 🐾

Group – Utility
Country of origin – Japan
Originally bred as a fighting dog

This, the largest of all Japanese dogs, is a powerful, muscular dog of the spitz type, and can be easily recognised by his sheer size and his almost bear-like coat, which is thick and coarse with a soft, dense undercoat – and, of course, by his bushy tail held over his back. This is a dog who is best suited to experienced, strong owners who understand the importance of both training and socialising such a strong, stubborn and potentially highly territorial dog. The Akita is not an ideal family pet – mainly because while they are generally very good with their 'own' children, they can be highly protective, and can mistake boisterous games with other children for a threat and take unwanted action. For an owner who understands this breed, the Akita will show unwavering loyalty and, while they are not affectionate dogs and do not show their feelings, their bond to their owner is unquestionable. Once they gain respect for their owner, they are easily trained and are reportedly very easy to toilet train, being almost cat-like in their cleanliness.

HOUSE

AMERICAN COCKER SPANIEL

Height	34–39cm
How much exercise?	🐾 🐾 🐾 🐾
How easy to train?	🐾 🐾 🐾 🐾
How noisy?	🐾 🐾 🐾
How much grooming?	🐾 🐾 🐾
How rare?	🐾 🐾 🐾 🐾

Group – Gundog
Country of origin – United States
Originally bred to flush and retrieve game birds

The American Cocker Spaniel is a smaller, showier version of his English cousin, and while he has a shorter nose and a more domed head, they share the same long ears, heavily feathered body and silky, medium to long length coat. This is a happy, joyful little dog who loves to play and is always busy. The American Cocker Spaniel is a pleasure to train and he can excel at anything he puts his mind to, but despite his merry nature he can be rather stubborn! However, he does make an ideal pet, being affectionate with all the family. This is a breed for owners who love grooming as he also loves plenty of exercise including diving into the undergrowth – and bringing lots of it back into the house with him! While he is friendly with everybody, the American Cocker Spaniel needs plenty of socialisation to prevent him becoming shy, and also lots of training to prevent him being possessive of toys or food.

HOUSE

BASSET HOUND

Height	33–38cm
How much exercise?	🐾 🐾 🐾
How easy to train?	🐾
How noisy?	🐾 🐾
How much grooming?	🐾 🐾
How rare?	🐾 🐾 🐾

Group – Hound
Country of origin – France
Originally bred for tracking

Thanks to advertising campaigns for shoes and other products, this long-eared, droopy-eyed, short-legged hound with his short, smooth coat has become instantly recognisable all over the world. The Basset Hound is a gentle, placid, rather solemn dog who is friendly to everyone he meets – and he seems to melt the hardest of hearts! He makes an enchanting family dog – although he still needs a fair bit of steady exercise. This isn't a dog for someone who wants obedience, however, as the Basset Hound is both independent and spectacularly stubborn. He is also 'nose-led' and so if he smells something interesting when out on walks, he will pursue it with determination, dragging the owner behind! Grooming him is a simple matter thanks to his short coat, but keeping his long ears clean is important.

HOUSE

BEAGLE

Height	33–40cm
How much exercise?	🐾 🐾 🐾 🐾
How easy to train?	🐾 🐾
How noisy?	🐾 🐾 🐾
How much grooming?	🐾
How rare?	🐾 🐾

Group – Hounds
Country of origin – England
Originaly bred as a pack hound

The Beagle is probably the best-known and best-loved of all the hounds, and is easily recognised by his medium-sized, compact shape, his cheerful personality, his waving tail and his short, often tri-coloured, coat. This is a happy, easy-going dog who is full of life and fun to be around. The Beagle loves everyone, is delighted to join in any family activity and will enjoy as much exercise as anyone will give him. He is, however, a challenge to train as, like most hounds, he is at heart an independent soul – and following a scent will be far more interesting and important to him than following commands. He may never be reliable off the lead, but he still needs plenty of free-running exercise, so owners need to have plenty of outdoor space. Grooming is an easy job thanks to his short coat. However, his hairs do seem to get everywhere!

HOUSE

BEARDED COLLIE

Height	51–56cm
How much exercise?	🐾 🐾 🐾 🐾
How easy to train?	🐾 🐾 🐾 🐾
How noisy?	🐾 🐾 🐾
How much grooming?	🐾 🐾 🐾 🐾 🐾
How rare?	🐾 🐾 🐾 🐾

Group – Pastoral
Country of origin – Scotland
Originally bred for driving cows and herding sheep

This is a medium- to large-sized shaggy dog with a long, thick, harsh top coat and a furry undercoat. The Bearded Collie (or Beardie) is the clown of the collie world, being both playful and exuberant, but if trained and his enthusiasm channelled into work, he can still excel in any of the canine sports. The Beardie needs an active, sensitive owner with plenty of time on their hands both to train and play with their hairy companion, and also to stay on top of the endless grooming. They shouldn't be too house-proud either as with a Beardie a lot of the great outdoors can end up indoors! With their love of play and games, Bearded Collies make ideal family dogs, as long as they are both well-trained and get enough exercise to curb their boundless enthusiasm, which can lead to smaller children being knocked over by an over-exuberant Beardie-bounce.

HOUSE

BERNESE MOUNTAIN DOG

Height	58–70cm
How much exercise?	🐾 🐾 🐾
How easy to train?	🐾 🐾 🐾
How noisy?	🐾 🐾
How much grooming?	🐾 🐾 🐾 🐾
How rare?	🐾 🐾 🐾 🐾

Group – Working
Country of origin – Switzerland
Originally bred to pull carts

The Bernese Mountain Dog is a huge, friendly bear of a dog, and is easily recognisable thanks to both his size and his thick, medium-length, silky, shiny tricolour coat with white chest, paws and tail tip. This is a dog who needs plenty of space in the house (especially as his ever-wagging tail is at coffee table height!) and a good-sized garden to play in. He takes a lot of grooming as his coat is thick and takes a long time to dry when wet. He is an excellent family dog as he is a real gentle giant and loves everyone, but he can also unwittingly knock smaller children over! The Bernese Mountain Dog needs a fairly experienced owner – just because he is such a large dog and so must be trained to have manners. He makes a perfect dog for those with the space and time to look after him, play with him and give him the exercise, training and companionship he needs, and who can cope with his often tragically short life span.

HOUSE

BICHON FRISE

Height	**23–28cm**
How much exercise?	🐾 🐾
How easy to train?	🐾 🐾 🐾
How noisy?	🐾 🐾
How much grooming?	🐾 🐾 🐾 🐾
How rare?	🐾 🐾

Group – Toy
Country of Origin – Spain (Tenerife)
Originally bred as a companion to the nobility

The Bichon Frise is a small, white companion dog with a fine silky coat with corkscrew curls that takes daily grooming to keep in good condition. This is a good-natured dog who makes an ideal pet – especially for first time dog owners. He is happy, enjoys company and will get on with all the family (and loves playing games). However, he is not just a pampered lapdog – in fact he is also clever and can be trained to do virtually anything that his size will allow, including mini agility, and will enjoy doing so. The Bichon Frise will excel with an affectionate owner who will give him the human company he needs – and who will groom him daily. Like many of the companion breeds, he may not be happy being left alone for any length of time (and owners should work on this so it doesn't become a problem), but luckily he is small enough and friendly enough to accompany his owner on most outings.

HOUSE

BLOODHOUND

Height	58–69cm
How much exercise?	🐾 🐾 🐾
How easy to train?	🐾
How noisy?	🐾 ❙
How much grooming?	🐾 🐾
How rare?	🐾 🐾 🐾 🐾 🐾

Group – Hound
Country of origin – Belgium
Originally bred for tracking large game

The Bloodhound is probably the dog everyone thinks of when they imagine a tracking scenthound, and he certainly looks the part with his long droopy ears, large jowls, solemn expression, waving tail and short, smooth, black and tan, or liver and tan, coat. This dog is an absolute tracking master and is often described as a nose with a dog attached! As such, smells are very important to him. Any potential owner needs to include scent work in their routine, and give him plenty of chance to use his formidable nose. Like all hounds, training is not one of his priorities, and so he is unlikely to be safe off-lead. He needs plenty of steady exercise though, so owners need to be prepared for very long walks, being dragged around following their dog's nose! The Bloodhound is friendly to everyone he meets and is a real gentle giant, although, as the largest of the scent hounds, he may be too big and clumsy for small children.

HOUSE

BORDER COLLIE

Height	**46–54cm**
How much exercise?	🐾 🐾 🐾 🐾 🐾
How easy to train?	🐾 🐾 🐾 🐾 🐾
How noisy?	🐾 🐾 🐾 🐾
How much grooming?	🐾 🐾 🐾
How rare?	🐾 🐾

Group – Pastoral
Country of origin – Scottish borders
Originally bred for working sheep

The Border Collie is a medium-sized dog with a thick, medium-length top coat and a soft, dense undercoat to keep him warm in all weathers. He is the Einstein of the dog world, and virtually every obedience champion, agility winner and flyball wizard is a Border Collie. This is a dog who was born to work and be active every minute of every day and who needs an active, experienced and sensitive owner who will give him a job to do and an outlet for his endless energy and desire to chase and herd. For anyone who wants to compete in any of the canine sports, this is probably the perfect breed. By nature, the Border Collie is a relentless herder, and so will try and round up children, other pets and indeed anything he can find. A Border Collie who is not given a suitable outlet for his passion for work can resort to undesirable behaviour such as aggression, destructive behaviour, nuisance barking and be totally manic around the house. Border Collies form very strong bonds with their owners.

HOUSE

BORDER TERRIER

Height	25–28cm
How much exercise?	🐾 🐾 🐾
How easy to train?	🐾 🐾 🐾
How noisy?	🐾 🐾 🐾
How much grooming?	🐾 🐾
How rare?	🐾

Group – Terrier
Country of Origin – England
Originally bred to work with foxhounds by flushing foxes out of their lairs

The Border Terrier is a frequently seen dog, and is easily recognisable with his harsh, dense, weatherproof coat, his compact body and his otter-like, whiskery face. This is one of the easier terriers to own as he is, on the whole, a playful, fun-loving dog who is affectionate to his family – including children – and sociable with strangers. As he was originally bred to work with foxhounds, he tends to be friendlier with other dogs than many of the terrier breeds, but he still needs socialising. He will be equally happy lazing by the fire as he will be on long country walks, but he still needs plenty of exercise. He also needs daily brushing to get rid of all the loose hairs that will otherwise end up all over the furniture! The Border Terrier is a great introduction to terrier breeds, being less feisty, less noisy and less argumentative than many, and will be happy to join in any family games or canine sports. Watch out for the cat though!

HOUSE

BORZOI

Height	**68–74cm**
How much exercise?	🐾 🐾 🐾
How easy to train?	🐾
How noisy?	🐾
How much grooming?	🐾 🐾 🐾 🐾
How rare?	🐾 🐾 🐾 🐾 🐾

Group – Hound
Country of origin – Russia
Originally bred as ceremonial wolf-hunting hounds

The Borzoi is a rarely seen dog, but, as a true Russian aristocrat, once seen he is never forgotten with his long Roman nose, heavily-feathered, tall, rangy body and his long, fine wavy coat. This is a head-turning, traffic-stoppingly elegant dog, who is ideal for owners who don't want or expect obedience but who appreciate this free spirit of the dog world. Training is most definitely beneath a Borzoi and as such he will probably never be reliable off-lead (except in enclosed areas) as the thrill of the chase and the joy of running are too strong. He needs daily grooming to keep his long coat tangle free. In the home this is a relaxed, quiet and gentle dog, who is affectionate to his owner, and highly sensitive, although aloof or haughtily indifferent with strangers.

HOUSE

BOSTON TERRIER

Height	**38–42cm**
How much exercise?	🐾 🐾
How easy to train?	🐾 🐾 🐾
How noisy?	🐾 🐾
How much grooming?	🐾
How rare?	🐾 🐾 🐾 🐾 🐾

Group – Utility
Country of origin – United States
Originally bred for fighting

Despite their very distant history as fighting dogs, Boston Terriers are friendly, good-natured dogs and certainly attract attention wherever they go with their flat faces, big eyes, bat-like ears, no tail and short, smooth, easy-to-care-for coat. Even though he is called a terrier, he isn't at all terrier-like in nature, and he would far rather be at home with his owner than getting into the usual terrier mischief. This is a real people dog – outgoing and sociable to all but especially loyal and affectionate to his owner. The Boston Terrier can be an active family dog and is easy to train (although sometimes stubborn), but he will also enjoy being a couch potato when the mood takes him. This is a smart, low-maintenance dog who makes an enchanting companion for those who like his rather unconventional looks.

HOUSE

BOUVIER DES FLANDERS

Height	59–68cm
How much exercise?	🐾 🐾 🐾 🐾 🐾
How easy to train?	🐾 🐾
How noisy?	🐾 🐾 🐾
How much grooming?	🐾 🐾 🐾
How rare?	🐾 🐾 🐾 🐾 🐾

Group – Working
Country of origin – Belgium
Originally bred as a cattle herder

While the Bouvier des Flanders isn't a common breed, once seen he is never forgotten as such a large, imposing, strong dog with thick, coarse, curly coat and a formidable beard definitely leaves a lasting impression. This is, without doubt, not a dog for everyone. He is both strong and active, is fiercely loyal to his family (including children) and often very protective of them, while often being problematical with strangers – both people and dogs. With the right owner who can socialise him, has the strength and experience to handle and train him, and the time to exercise this powerhouse of a dog, he can excel in any of the canine sports, including agility, or work in virtually any capacity – and make a fabulous, if challenging, companion.

HOUSE

BOXER

Height	53–63cm
How much exercise?	🐾 🐾 🐾 🐾 🐾
How easy to train?	🐾 🐾 🐾 🐾
How noisy?	🐾 🐾
How much grooming?	🐾
How rare?	🐾

Group – Working
Country of origin – Germany
Originally bred as a guard dog

This is another dog that everyone recognises. The Boxer is the tallest of the flat-faced dogs, and this, coupled with his elegant athletic shape and his short, smooth coat makes him totally distinctive and unmistakable. Despite the Boxer's guarding and hunting past, he makes an excellent, low-maintenance (in terms of grooming, not exercise!) family pet – although his sheer exuberance and love of life may be too much for smaller children. This is a breed that loves people (although he should be socialised with strangers), enjoys all kinds of games and will excel at training classes or agility. The Boxer will thrive on endless exercise, as this is a high-energy dog who does everything at top speed! While the Boxer loves people, he may not be so keen on other dogs, and so lots of socialisation is vital. With an active, experienced owner who enjoys training and plenty of exercise, the Boxer can make an ideal, devoted companion and lifelong friend.

HOUSE

BULLDOG

Height	31–36cm
How much exercise?	🐾
How easy to train?	🐾
How noisy?	🐾
How much grooming?	🐾
How rare?	🐾

Group – Utility
Country of origin – England
Originally bred for bull-baiting

This is a dog who needs no introduction – everybody recognises him instantly. Everyone also seems totally divided on whether he is ugly or stunning (or a combination of both!) with his large head, flat face, undershot jaw, short legs, piggy tail, short smooth coat and rolling body. Despite his bull-baiting past, this breed has been transformed into a gentle companion dog with a good nature and a large degree of couch potato-ness! This has come at a price though, and exercise is difficult with his short legs, ungainly body and his flat face and very short nose, which makes breathing difficult, especially in hot weather. As such, this is not a dog for people who enjoy long walks – a Bulldog's idea of exercise is walking to his food bowl! Every now and then, his past shines through, and this is a dog who needs plenty of socialisation if he is to get on with other dogs. A Bulldog's idea of heaven is somewhere comfortable to sleep, plenty of food and an owner who can provide a good tummy rub (and who doesn't mind snoring).

HOUSE

BULL TERRIER

Height	53–56cm
How much exercise?	🐾 🐾 🐾
How easy to train?	🐾
How noisy?	🐾
How much grooming?	🐾
How rare?	🐾

Group – Terrier
Country of origin – England
Originally bred for dog fighting

Love him or hate him, you can't mistake this dog, with his famous egg-shaped head, Roman nose, slightly piggy eyes, and short, flat coat. He is a hugely affectionate family pet, although he often thinks he is a lapdog! The Bull Terrier needs plenty of early socialisation with other dogs (and continued care) so that he doesn't become aggressive with them. He will probably never be reliable with cats or small animals. Training a Bull Terrier is without doubt a huge challenge as they are not the brightest dogs, and they see no point at all in doing what someone tells them! Sadly, this is a breed that has become a status symbol for macho types whose irresponsibility has brought the breed into disrepute. However, a well-socialised, sensibly handled Bull Terrier with an experienced owner is a delight to be around – as long as you have a sense of humour!

HOUSE

CAIRN TERRIER

Height	28–31cm
How much exercise?	🐾 🐾 🐾
How easy to train?	🐾 🐾 🐾
How noisy?	🐾 🐾 🐾 🐾
How much grooming?	🐾 🐾
How rare?	🐾 🐾

Group – Terrier
Country of Origin – Scotland
Originally bred to hunt vermin

The Cairn Terrier is a small, rather scruffy but very endearing little dog who has a harsh outer coat with a short, soft undercoat to protect him from all weathers. Despite being one of the smallest of the terriers, the Cairn is a feisty, courageous, confident dog who is endlessly inquisitive and always on the go. He is devoted to his family and friendly to strangers – both human and dog, but is quick to defend himself, even from much larger dogs, if he feels it is necessary. This is another of the terriers who may never be reliable with cats or small animals as his hunting instinct is still strong. Owners need to have a sense of humour, not mind a bit of noise and like lots of exercise to enjoy life with this happy but sometimes stubborn dog.

HOUSE

CARDIGAN WELSH CORGI

Height	30cm
How much exercise?	🐾 🐾 🐾
How easy to train?	🐾 🐾
How noisy?	🐾 🐾 🐾
How much grooming?	🐾 🐾
How rare?	🐾 🐾 🐾 🐾 🐾

Group – Pastoral
Country of origin – Wales
Originally bred for driving cattle

The Cardigan Welsh Corgi and the Pembroke Welsh Corgi are very similar; in fact it wasn't until 1927 that they were shown at Crufts as separate breeds. However, there are differences, the main one being that the Cardigan has a long, bushy tail and larger, rounded ears. They are also generally darker in colour than the Pembroke and slightly larger, heavier and longer, and are often much more easy going. Despite this, they are still very much 'big personalities in a small body'. The Cardigan Welsh Corgi needs an experienced, relaxed owner who will channel this dog's working abilities into play, training and games, and not into biting ankles (either in play or as a means to get rid of the postman!). This is another breed that needs well socialising with as many different people (and children if they are to live with them) and other dogs as possible, as they can be reserved with strangers and utterly fearless when faced with much larger dogs.

HOUSE

CAVALIER KING CHARLES SPANIEL

Height	**31–33cm**
How much exercise?	🐾 🐾 🐾
How easy to train?	🐾 🐾 🐾 🐾 🐾
How noisy?	🐾 🐾
How much grooming?	🐾 🐾 🐾
How rare?	🐾

Group – Toy
Country of Origin – England
Originally bred as a companion

This delightful companion dog is one of the larger of the toy breeds, and looks very much the Spaniel with his long, silky coat complete with plenty of feathering that will require daily grooming. Of all the many breeds of dog, the Cavalier King Charles Spaniel is probably one of the best for first-time dog owners, families and indeed anyone who wants a happy, playful, affectionate, undemanding yet active companion. He is easy to train, easy to live with and is intelligent enough to excel in obedience, mini agility or any of the canine sports that his owners may wish to try their hand at. This is a breed who should also be happy to live with cats and any other pets. However, he is a gentle dog and so may not be happy in a boisterous, noisy family. The Cavalier King Charles Spaniel will need more exercise than many of the other toy breeds, both to keep him happy, and to stop him getting fat (something the breed can be prone to).

HOUSE

CHIHUAHUA

Height	15–23cm
How much exercise?	🐾
How easy to train?	🐾 🐾 🐾
How noisy?	🐾 🐾
How much grooming?	🐾
How rare?	🐾 🐾 🐾 🐾

Group – Toy
Country of Origin – Mexico
Originally bred as a comforter and companion

The Chihuahua is famous for being the smallest dog in the world, and with his tiny body, domed head, big eyes and smooth, soft coat, he is probably one of the most recognisable. There is also a long-coated version of the breed which is just as tiny! However, what a Chihuahua lacks in size, he certainly makes up for in character. His diminutive size means that this is a dog that has to be carefully looked after – especially as a puppy – as he is easily injured, so he shouldn't live with boisterous small children or larger dogs. Many Chihuahuas are treated as fashion accessories or toys by owners who insist on carrying them around in bags. This isn't fair on the dog (who is still a dog and not a toy) and also not fair on people who meet him, as his spirited character, coupled with a sense of self-importance arising from being constantly carried around, can lead him to use his small but surprisingly accurate teeth!

HOUSE

CHOW CHOW

Height	46–56cm
How much exercise?	🐾
How easy to train?	🐾
How noisy?	🐾
How much grooming?	🐾 🐾 🐾 🐾
How rare?	🐾 🐾 🐾 🐾 🐾

Group – Utility
Country or origin – China
Originally bred for food, but also worked as a guard,
hunting dog and sledge puller

The Chow Chow is a large bear-like dog with a thick, abundant topcoat and a woolly undercoat. They come in a variety of colours and while the most popular is red, they can also be black, cream, blue and cinnamon. The Chow Chow is a fascinating dog to live with, but is very aloof and reserved, is both stubborn and independent, is not playful, and in general neither gives nor likes affection (and may actively object to it!). He also hates being told off. With strangers he can be territorial, and with other dogs he may be a real problem. His thick coat also means that in hot weather he can overheat, which increases his irritability. He is the original grumpy old man, although if you were originally bred for the cooking pot, you might not be that happy either! This is a breed for an experienced owner who likes their dogs to be independent and with little desire to please – in fact almost like a cat!

HOUSE

DACHSHUND

Height	13–16cm
How much exercise?	🐾
How easy to train?	🐾 🐾
How noisy?	🐾 🐾 🐾
How much grooming?	🐾
How rare?	🐾 🐾

Ratings for Miniature Short-haired Dachshund

Group – Hound
Country of origin – Germany
Originally bred to dig out rabbits or foxes from their burrows

There are six different types of Dachshund – long-haired, wire-haired and smooth-haired, with standard and miniature versions of each – but they all have the same characteristic long backs and short legs that make them so recognisable. In personality the Dachshund is a little like a cross between a hound and a terrier. They are tough little dogs, can be independent and 'selectively obedient' but also are often busy, inquisitive and into everything. Their working history often rears its head, and owners shouldn't be surprised to find tunnels appearing in the garden as these dogs like to dig! Of all the varieties, the long-haireds seem to be the most laid-back, and the wire-haireds the most outgoing. The smooth-haireds may be the most feisty, especially with strangers (dog or human). All need plenty of socialising and some may never be safe with the neighbour's cat! Grooming also depends on type, with smooth-haireds needing hardly any, and long-haireds needing a daily brush.

HOUSE

DALMATIAN

Height	56–61cm
How much exercise?	🐾 🐾 🐾 🐾 🐾
How easy to train?	🐾 🐾 🐾 ᕯ
How noisy?	🐾 🐾 🐾
How much grooming?	🐾 🐾 ᕯ
How rare?	🐾 🐾

Group – Utility
Country of origin – England
Originally bred as a carriage dog (especially associated with horse-drawn fire engines)

This may well be the most famous breed in the world, and everyone recognises this tall, elegant, short-haired dog immediately due to his film appearances and the fact that he is the only truly spotted dog in the world. The Dalmatian was bred to run alongside carriages, either to protect the contents and travellers (originally from highwaymen) or to show the high status of his owners. This means that the Dalmatian was quite literally born to run, and still needs almost endless exercise. If they get enough exercise, they make quiet, affectionate house dogs who will be devoted to the whole family (if raised with sensible children). If they don't get enough exercise, they will be escapologists who don't come back when called and who hurtle around the house like a whirlwind! Despite their short coat, they need a lot of grooming to get rid of loose coat, and their white spiky hairs get into everything (and seem to never come out!). Owners need to be prepared to never wear black again!

HOUSE

DANDIE DINMONT TERRIER

Height	20–28cm
How much exercise?	🐾 🐾
How easy to train?	🐾 🐾 🐾
How noisy?	🐾 🐾
How much grooming?	🐾 🐾 🐾
How rare?	🐾 🐾 🐾 🐾 🐾

Group – Terrier
Country of origin – Scotland
Originally bred to kill vermin (especially rodents)

The Dandie Dinmont Terrier is one of the most enchanting-looking of all terriers with his long low body, short legs, and coat of hard top hair and linty undercoat. His most distinctive feature however is his topknot, which makes him look a bit as if he is wearing a fluffy crash helmet. He has a more relaxed personality than many terrier breeds, and he will get on well with all the family (as long as any children are well-trained!) – although small animals and the neighbour's cat may not be quite as safe. He is, in general, a fairly laid-back character, and is loyal and affectionate to his owners. If pushed, however, he will most certainly stand his ground and so needs plenty of early socialisation to make sure he is relaxed around other dogs. With strangers he can be quite reserved, and his heart has to be won… it isn't just given away! He is not a noisy dog, but when he does bark, the woof sounds as if it comes from a much larger dog.

HOUSE

DOBERMANN

Height	65–69cm
How much exercise?	🐾 🐾 🐾 🐾 🐾
How easy to train?	🐾 🐾 🐾
How noisy?	🐾 🐾 🐾
How much grooming?	🐾
How rare?	🐾

Group – Working
Country of origin – Germany
Originally bred as a guard dog and bodyguard

Everybody recognises the Dobermann, having seen him portrayed in endless TV programmes and films as the ultimate guard dog! He certainly looks the part with his tall aristocratic looks, his long nose and his smooth, short, glossy, often black and tan, coat. This is another dog that isn't suited to first-time owners, or those of a more gentle, unassertive disposition. This is a large, powerful dog, who needs sensitive, fair but firm handling, and lots of socialisation to help him fulfil his massive potential. A well-trained, well-socialised Dobermann is a fabulous dog capable of virtually anything. A Dobermann who isn't trained and socialised is, as best, a nuisance and, at worst, a downright danger. The Dobermann is loyal and affectionate to his owners, but may be suspicious of strangers – people and dogs. With the right owner, he is easy to train, responsive and can excel in obedience. This is very much a working dog and he flourishes with a job to do.

HOUSE

ENGLISH COCKER SPANIEL

Height	38–41cm
How much exercise?	🐾 🐾 🐾 🐾
How easy to train?	🐾 🐾 🐾 🐾
How noisy?	🐾 🐾 🐾
How much grooming?	🐾 🐾 🐾
How rare?	🐾

Group – Gundog
Country of origin – England
Originally bred to flush and retrieve game birds

The Cocker Spaniel is one of the most popular breeds of dog in the world, and rightly so. He is a good manageable size, and is easily recognised with his long ears, appealing eyes and silky, feathered coat. This is a happy, friendly active breed that is ideal for families so long as they enjoy a lot of exercise – this is not a dog for couch potatoes! These exuberant dogs both enjoy and need training as they can be quite wilful characters, and they can excel at agility (which is useful to burn off some of their excess energy). The Cocker Spaniel needs a daily brush to keep him looking tidy and to stop his coat tangling. With an energetic owner who enjoys training and grooming, the Cocker Spaniel makes one of the most perfect companion dogs. A bored one, however, is a nightmare! The Cocker Spaniel has an extraordinary nose and can excel in scent work as well as agility.

HOUSE

FLAT COATED RETRIEVER

Height	56–61cm
How much exercise?	🐾 🐾 🐾 🐾
How easy to train?	🐾 🐾 🐾 🐾
How noisy?	🐾 🐾
How much grooming?	🐾 🐾
How rare?	🐾 🐾

Group – Gundog
Country of origin – England
Originally bred to retrieve game

The Flat Coated Retriever is one of the rarer retrievers – in fact many people don't realise that this regal-looking, tall, black dog with a flat coat and feathered legs and tail, is part of the same family as the world's most popular breeds. This is a happy, sociable dog who makes an excellent pet for active families and even makes a good dog for first-time owners. He lives happily with other animals (whether of the canine or feline variety – as long as properly and sensibly introduced), is friendly with children, will welcome strangers, and will join in enthusiastically with any family activity. The Flat Coated Retriever is a joy to train and is responsive and willing, and as such he can excel in agility or any of the canine sports. His feathered coat needs a daily groom to keep it tangle-free, and, as a true outdoor dog, he does tend to bring a lot of the outdoors back indoors with him in terms of mud, twigs and bits of bush! For those with the energy to give this dog the exercise he needs, he is the perfect, devoted companion.

HOUSE

FRENCH BULLDOG

Height	30–31cm
How much exercise?	🐾
How easy to train?	🐾 🐾
How noisy?	🐾 🐾
How much grooming?	🐾
How rare?	🐾 🐾 🐾 🐾

Group – Utility
Country of origin – France
Originally bred as a companion

The French Bulldog is a fascinating-looking little dog who looks like a miniaturised but bat-eared bulldog, and has the same flat face, short tail and smooth, short coat, but in a much smaller package. This is a friendly, good-natured and playful dog, who makes an ideal companion or family dog, and is as happy living in towns and cities as he is in the countryside. His short, smooth coat needs little grooming and is easy to care for, but the folds across his nose will need cleaning every day. Like all flat-faced breeds, the French Bulldog can have breathing difficulties, and so not only can they not walk too far, they are also prone to overheating in the summer and snoring. Despite this they are active dogs in the house who love games with all the family. However, socialisation is important if he is to get on with other dogs.

HOUSE

GERMAN SHEPHERD DOG

Height	**58–63cm**
How much exercise?	🐾 🐾 🐾 🐾 🐾
How easy to train?	🐾 🐾 🐾 🐾 🐾
How noisy?	🐾 🐾 🐾 🐾
How much grooming?	🐾 🐾 🐾
How rare?	🐾

Group – Pastoral
Country of origin – Germany
Originally bred as a sheep-herding dog

The German Shepherd Dog (GSD) is one of the world's most popular dogs, to be found everywhere working as police dogs, guide dogs and guard dogs, as well as obedience and agility dogs. The GSD is a large, wolf-like dog with upright pointed ears, long nose, bushy tail and thick medium to long coat with a thick undercoat. This is a loyal and devoted dog who loves nothing more than being wherever his owner is. Sadly the popularity of the GSD has led to some irresponsible breeding, and as a result many now show a high degree of nervousness or even aggression. For an experienced, active, strong owner, who is prepared for plenty of training, exercise, socialisation and daily grooming – and who takes the time to get a puppy from a good breeder – the GSD is quite possibly the perfect dog. In inexperienced or incompetent hands, however, this can be a very scary dog indeed.

HOUSE

GOLDEN RETRIEVER

Height	**51–61cm**
How much exercise?	🐾 🐾 🐾 🐾
How easy to train?	🐾 🐾 🐾 🐾
How noisy?	🐾 🐾
How much grooming?	🐾 🐾 🐾
How rare?	🐾

Group – Gundog
Country of origin – Scotland
Originally bred to retrieve waterfowl

The Golden Retriever is one of the most popular of all dog breeds and everybody seems to know them and love them. They are certainly very recognisable with their ever-wagging tails, soft dark eyes, friendly expressions and wavy golden coats. For many people, this is the perfect breed. The Golden Retriever loves everyone and everything, which makes him ideal for most families, whether they have children, other dogs or cats. He is a joy to train, is willing and responsive, loves to please, and can excel in any sport or any job. This is a dog who needs plenty of exercise, though, as it is easy to forget that he is bred to work. The Golden Retriever is also a playful breed, enjoying games of all kinds and is often waiting for you at the door when you come home with something precious or expensive in his mouth! This is an affectionate dog who loves to be with people, whether it is walking miles in all weathers or just cuddling on the sofa.

HOUSE

GREAT DANE

Height	**71–76cm**
How much exercise?	🐾 🐾 🐾
How easy to train?	🐾 🐾 🐾
How noisy?	🐾
How much grooming?	🐾
How rare?	🐾 🐾

Group – Working
Country of origin – Germany
Originally bred as a property guard and then later to hunt large game

This is a true giant of the dog world, easily recognisable by his sheer size along with his short, dense but smooth coat. The Great Dane is a dog for a real enthusiast as it is a challenge to live with a dog whose nose is on cooker and work surface height, whose tail can clear a table with one powerful wag, and who is bigger and stronger than the average adult woman. Despite this, or more to the point because of it, the Great Dane is bred to be a gentle giant, but they are known for being clumsy, especially when young. They need plenty of training and socialising, as an owner of a dog of this size must be able to control him and ensure he is friendly and well behaved to all. This is a dog who needs a big house, a big garden and a big car – and an owner with a big bank balance!

HOUSE

GRIFFON BRUXELLOIS (BRUSSELS GRIFFON)

Height	18–20cm
How much exercise?	🐾 🐾 🐾
How easy to train?	🐾 🐾 🐾
How noisy?	🐾 🐾 🐾 🐾
How much grooming?	🐾 🐾
How rare?	🐾 🐾 🐾 🐾 🐾

Group – Toy
Country of origin – Belgium
Originally bred to kill rats before becoming a companion

The Griffon Bruxellois is one of the toy breeds that were originally bred to work, and so looks a bit like a cross between a workmanlike terrier and a monkey! They are small with a short, wiry, harsh coat and have a characteristic flat yet cheeky face. The working instincts of this breed mean that he is a playful, inquisitive and fun companion who will enjoy a good game as much, if not more, than a walk. However, these instincts also mean that he may not be safe with small animals! With his lively nature, he makes a good family pet, but is better suited to families with older or quieter children, as he can easily be injured by rough play. The Griffon Bruxellois is devoted to his owner and, while generally friendly with strangers, he will make a good watchdog as he is more than happy to use his voice! This is another breed that may not like to be left alone as they crave company.

HOUSE

IRISH SETTER

Height	64–69cm
How much exercise?	🐾 🐾 🐾 🐾 🐾
How easy to train?	🐾 🐾 🐾
How noisy?	🐾 🐾
How much grooming?	🐾 🐾 🐾
How rare?	🐾 🐾 🐾

Group – Gundog
Country of origin – Ireland
Originally bred for hunting birds

The Irish Setter is probably the most flamboyant of all the gundogs, and this tall, elegant dog with his soft brown eyes, and his blazing red coat certainly makes heads turn wherever he goes. This is a dog for the extremely active – an Irish Setter is always on the go, always busy and always alert, and so it takes an energetic owner to keep up with him and to keep him happy. He is a fabulous dog for very active families, as he loves everyone, is happy-go-lucky, and is friendly with children, other dogs and cats alike (although he may chase strange ones). Training an Irish Setter is a challenge, and he always rates very low in 'the most intelligent dog' lists! He isn't actually that stupid, his mind is just always racing and on other things! For people with time to exercise this dog, and space to let him burn off his almost endless energy, the Irish Setter makes a wonderful, affectionate and exuberant companion.

HOUSE

ITALIAN GREYHOUND

Height	32–38cm
How much exercise?	🐾 🐾 🐾
How easy to train?	🐾 🐾
How noisy?	🐾 🐾
How much grooming?	🐾
How rare?	🐾 🐾 🐾 🐾 🐾

Group – Toy
Country of origin – Italy
Originally bred as a companion

The Italian Greyhound is a perfect miniature of his much larger hunting and racing cousin, having the same fine, short coat that needs little grooming to look sleek and shiny. While this is ideal for those who like low-maintenance dogs, it does mean that he feels the cold, and will need a warm home, a cosy bed and maybe even a jumper! While the Italian Greyhound was bred as a companion, he still has all the instincts of a sighthound and may chase any small animal he spots on walks, and so can be difficult to recall. His size and delicate shape make him prone to injury and so he is not suited to life in a boisterous family or with young children – and, although he is stronger than he looks, he also seems to think himself indestructible and so often comes to grief jumping fearlessly from heights. This is a sweet-natured, very elegant and energetic dog who will be devoted and affectionate to his owner and probably fairly aloof to everyone else!

HOUSE

JACK RUSSELL/ PARSON RUSSELL

Height	33–36cm
How much exercise?	🐾 🐾 🐾 🐾
How easy to train?	🐾 🐾 🐾
How noisy?	🐾 🐾 🐾 🐾 🐾
How much grooming?	🐾 🐾
How rare?	🐾 🐾 🐾 🐾

Height and ratings for Parson Russell Terrier

Group – Terrier
Country of origin – England
Originally bred to help hunt foxes and kill vermin

While everybody thinks they know the Jack Russell Terrier, few people realise that the dog they know isn't the same one that the Kennel Club recognises! What people think of as a Jack Russell Terrier can be anything from a small, squat, short-legged, smooth-coated barrel of a dog all the way up to a much taller, slimmer, wiry-haired version – and indeed it is this latter model that is the KC recognised dog. This dog is called the Parson Russell Terrier to distinguish it from its 'non-recognised', but much more famous, cousins. The Jack Russell is probably the most terrier-like of all the terriers. He is tireless, feisty, noisy, inquisitive and crammed full of exuberant personality. He needs plenty of socialisation and training to make sure he is friendly with other dogs, people and children, and to make sure he comes back when called! However, small animals or the neighbour's cat may never be safe. This is an ideal dog for an active owner who likes plenty of character and activity in a small bundle.

HOUSE

JAPANESE CHIN

Height	23–25cm
How much exercise?	🐾
How easy to train?	🐾 🐾
How noisy?	🐾
How much grooming?	🐾 🐾 🐾
How rare?	🐾 🐾 🐾 🐾 🐾

Group – Toy
Country of origin – Japan
Originally bred as a lapdog for Japanese nobility

The Japanese Chin is an easily recognised, if fairly rarely seen, little dog. His short nose, bulbous eyes and high brow make him look permanently surprised, while his long, soft, straight, silky hair makes him look every inch the oriental aristocrat he was bred to be. The Japanese Chin makes an excellent companion and they are especially devoted to their owners – in fact are somewhat 'in your face' dogs, and will follow owners everywhere given half a chance. This can cause separation problems if forced to be apart from their humans, and this needs to be worked on. They need daily grooming to keep their luxurious coat in good condition, and they do shed quite a lot. This is a happy, entertaining dog, who is friendly to everyone he meets. However, he is a tiny, delicate dog who can be easily injured by boisterous play. The Japanese Chin also makes a good city dog as he is quiet, does not mind living in small spaces and needs little exercise.

HOUSE

JAPANESE SPITZ

Height	30–37cm
How much exercise?	🐾 🐾 🐾
How easy to train?	🐾 🐾 🐾
How noisy?	🐾 🐾 🐾 🐾 🐾
How much grooming?	🐾 🐾 🐾
How rare?	🐾 🐾 🐾 🐾 🐾

Group – Utility
Country of origin – Japan
Originally bred as a companion

In everything apart from size, the Japanese Spitz looks almost identical to his spitz cousin the Samoyed, with his foxy face, bushy tail held over his back, and his thick white topcoat with profuse undercoat, which takes some serious grooming to keep in good, healthy condition. This is a bold and lively dog who, despite his size, makes a very good watchdog, and tends to be aloof and reserved with strangers. Once they have made a friend though, they will be friends for life. With their owners they are loyal and affectionate, and enjoy lots of play and exercise. Once motivated, the Japanese Spitz can be surprisingly trainable and some excel in agility and obedience. With good socialisation, he will be good with children and other animals, and will happily get along with all the family. Training is also needed to prevent him becoming a very noisy dog who loves the sound of his own voice and wants to make sure everybody else hears it too!

HOUSE

KERRY BLUE TERRIER

Height	44–48cm
How much exercise?	🐾 🐾 🐾 🐾
How easy to train?	🐾 🐾 ⸰
How noisy?	🐾 🐾 🐾
How much grooming?	🐾 🐾 🐾
How rare?	🐾 🐾 🐾 🐾 🐾

Group – Terrier
Country of origin – Ireland
Originally bred to kill rats and hunt otters

The Kerry Blue Terrier is very distinctive looking dog, and, although not seen often, he is easily recognisable by his long face, beard and non-shedding, blue-shaded coat of soft wavy hair. This terrier is a bit of a Jekyll and Hyde character – being loving, devoted and playful with his owners and people he knows, and anything from suspicious to very unfriendly with people he doesn't! He needs a lot of early socialisation to try and encourage him to get on with other dogs, and he needs plenty of firm but fair and sensitive training to allow him to get all the free-running exercise he needs. This is a dog who will hunt and kill small animals – and may never get on with the cat! With an experienced and dedicated owner, this is a dog who is capable of anything from obedience to tracking.

HOUSE

LABRADOR RETRIEVER

Height	55–57cm
How much exercise?	🐾 🐾 🐾 🐾
How easy to train?	🐾 🐾 🐾 🐾 🐾
How noisy?	🐾 🐾
How much grooming?	🐾 🐾
How rare?	🐾

Group – Gundog
Country of origin – Canada
Originally bred as a water retriever

The Labrador Retriever is the most popular breed of dog in the world, and as such everybody recognises him with his ever-wagging otter-like tail, soft brown eyes and his short smooth, coat that comes in either yellow, black or chocolate colours. The Labrador Retriever makes an ideal first dog for families and individuals so long as they are active and energetic. He can be a greedy dog, and that, coupled with the life of a couch potato, will quickly lead to a fat dog. This is a dog who loves everybody and everything – he loves people, loves children, loves other dogs and loves life! He will even learn to love the cat! He does need daily grooming though as those short hairs get everywhere! The Labrador Retriever is a joy to train, as he is responsive, willing and eager to please. He can easily excel in any canine sport, in any job – or just as the most enthusiastic and happy member of the family.

HOUSE

LAKELAND TERRIER

Height	33–37cm
How much exercise?	🐾 🐾 🐾 🐾
How easy to train?	🐾 🐾 🐾
How noisy?	🐾 🐾 🐾 🐾
How much grooming?	🐾 🐾
How rare?	🐾 🐾 🐾 🐾 🐾

Group – Terrier
Country of origin – England
Originally bred for killing vermin and helping hunt foxes

The Lakeland Terrier is often difficult to tell apart from some of the other similar looking terriers (he looks a lot like the Welsh Terrier but smaller), and it often takes an expert to recognise him from his alert expression, his business-like look and his harsh weather-resistant coat that has a good undercoat to protect him when working in all weathers. The Lakeland Terrier is an active, busy dog who needs plenty to do and endless exercise to keep him happy and easy to live with. He gets on better with other dogs than many of the terriers, but still needs a lot of socialisation to make him truly social. The Lakeland Terrier gets on well with sensible older children, but probably not the cat! For active owners with a sense of humour, who understand and are able to motivate terriers, this breed makes a great companion.

HOUSE

LEONBERGER

Height	65–80cm
How much exercise?	🐾 🐾 🐾 🐾
How easy to train?	🐾 🐾 🐾
How noisy?	🐾 🐾 🐾
How much grooming?	🐾 🐾 🐾 🐾
How rare?	🐾 🐾 🐾 🐾 🐾

Group – Working
Country of origin – Germany
Originally bred as a guard dog

The Leonberger is a rarely seen giant of a dog, but once seen he certainly makes an impression with his lion-like looks and thick medium-length hair complete with a mane at his chest and throat. This is a breed for an enthusiast – just because of the sheer size of this somewhat self-confident dog, and because he can weigh more than an adult woman! Any dog of this size must be well-trained and well socialised, just so he can be kept under control, and the Leonberger is no exception. His temperament, however, is generally good-natured and friendly, and he is devoted to his family (although his size can be intimidating for smaller children who he can easily knock over). The Leonberger needs an experienced, strong, active owner with plenty of time for training, socialising, grooming, playing and exercising to keep him healthy, happy and content. He is also a good and enthusiastic swimmer so owners need to watch out for lakes and rivers as this is a dog who takes a long time to dry!

MALTESE

Height	20–25cm
How much exercise?	🐾 🐾
How easy to train?	🐾 🐾
How noisy?	🐾 🐾 🐾 🐾
How much grooming?	🐾 🐾 🐾 🐾
How rare?	🐾 🐾 🐾 🐾 🐾

Group – Toy
Country of Origin – Malta
Originally bred as a companion

The Maltese is the ultimate in luxurious lapdogs with his long, straight, flowing, white hair, which is a challenge for all but the most dedicated of groomers to keep spotlessly clean and healthy – especially as this is an active little dog who loves exercise. This is a lively and alert companion dog who is friendly and affectionate to everyone he meets – although he can be surprisingly feisty if the need arises, especially with larger dogs. He loves being with his owner and is happy to be a lapdog – as long as he gets plenty of games to play as well. The Maltese is another very tiny dog who is not suited to life in a young or boisterous family. Instead he likes a quiet gentle owner who will spend time grooming and playing with him. Generally the hair of a Maltese has to be tied up on the top of his head with a ribbon so that he can see where he is going!

HOUSE

MINIATURE PINSCHER

Height	25–30cm
How much exercise?	🐾 🐾 🐾
How easy to train?	🐾 🐾
How noisy?	🐾 🐾 🐾
How much grooming?	🐾
How rare?	🐾 🐾 🐾 🐾 🐾

Group – Toy
Country of origin – Germany
Originally bred to kill rats

The Miniature Pinscher is another one of those companion dogs who have never forgotten their working roots. With his short black and tan, easy-to-care-for coat and his flamboyant movement, he looks every bit the ratter that he was bred to be – and also very similar to his much larger Pinscher cousins like the Dobermann. This is a breed who is constantly on the go and whose curiosity will ensure they are into everything. They are the typical 'big dog in a small body' and seem to have no idea that they aren't as large, if not larger, than other dogs they meet! They are affectionate with their owners, although still fairly independent, but need to be well socialised with strangers and other dogs. They will chase and can injure small animals, so care must be taken. The Miniature Pinscher is not an ideal family dog as he is easily injured and has little patience with children. He needs an active owner who is used to terrier-type dogs and who will keep him occupied.

HOUSE

MINIATURE & TOY POODLE

Height	28–38cm*/under 28cm**
How much exercise?	🐾 🐾 🐾
How easy to train?	🐾 🐾 🐾 🐾
How noisy?	🐾 🐾 🐾
How much grooming?	🐾 🐾 🐾 🐾
How rare?	🐾 🐾 🐾 🐾

*Miniature Poodle **Toy Poodle

Group – Utility
Country of origin – Germany
Originally bred as companions

The Miniature and Toy Poodles were developed as exact miniatures of the Standard Poodle and so have the same long pointy nose, flamboyant attitude and dense, non-shedding wavy coat. In attitude, these smaller Poodles are very similar to their bigger cousin. They need less exercise and less space, but are still just as active, alert and trainable. Perhaps because they are smaller and so feel slightly more vulnerable, they need more socialisation with strangers – dogs and human, so they are not wary of either. Again, because of their size, they are better with older children, as younger ones can be too boisterous for them. Like their Standard cousins, they need regular clipping as their hair grows continuously and doesn't shed. These smaller Poodles have often been employed as working dogs, and many Hearing Dogs for Deaf People are Miniature or Toy Poodles, or Poodle crosses. These bouncy, plucky little dogs also excel at mini agility.

HOUSE

MINIATURE SCHNAUZER

Height	33–36cm
How much exercise?	🐾 🐾 🐾
How easy to train?	🐾 🐾 🐾 🐾
How noisy?	🐾 🐾 🐾 🐾
How much grooming?	🐾 🐾 🐾
How rare?	🐾

Group – Utility
Country of origin – Germany
Originally bred as a ratter

The Miniature Schnauzer is an exact miniature of the larger schnauzers and so has the same characteristic bushy eyebrows, moustache and whiskers, and the wiry black, or salt and pepper coat that they all share. As the larger schnauzers that this dog originated from were originally herding or working dogs, the Miniature Schnauzer has inherited their trainability and this is a dog that can excel in any of the canine sports and will even compete in obedience if owners are so inclined. The Miniature Schnauzer's coat does not shed, which means he is easy to care for, but he will need a daily brush and also regular trimming every six to eight weeks. With good socialisation, he will get on with children and other dogs (although watch him with small animals and cats) and so will make a good and enthusiastic family pet, as long as the family likes a lot of exercise to keep this busy little dog happy and healthy, and doesn't mind a bit of noise!

HOUSE

NEWFOUNDLAND

Height	**66–71cm**
How much exercise?	🐾 🐾 🐾
How easy to train?	🐾 🐾 🐾
How noisy?	🐾 🐾
How much grooming?	🐾 🐾 🐾 🐾
How rare?	🐾 🐾 🐾

Group – Working
Country of origin – Canada
Originally bred to pull carts, help fishermen and for water rescue

This breed has often been described as a 'huge cuddly bear of a dog' and it is easy to see why. This is another giant of the dog world, and he comes complete with a huge medium length, dense, slightly oily coat with a vast, thick undercoat to protect him both from the cold and from the water he loves – and he has webbed feet. Newfoundlands are real gentle giants with a calm, good-natured personality, and are the real softies of the dog world, although they are often not aware of their own size and so can easily knock over smaller children or squash owners in an attempt to be a lapdog! This is a dog who loves the water and for whom swimming is probably his greatest joy. Owners should both recognise this and give him an outlet for his passion, as he finds exercising in water far easier than on land. The Newfoundland needs an owner who enjoys grooming, has plenty of space, and who is prepared to train him (because he is so large) and who has the physical strength to control such a big dog.

HOUSE

NORFOLK TERRIER

Height	24–25cm
How much exercise?	🐾 🐾 🐾
How easy to train?	🐾 🐾 🐾
How noisy?	🐾 🐾 🐾
How much grooming?	🐾 🐾
How rare?	🐾 🐾 🐾 🐾

Group – Terrier
Country of origin – England
Originally bred to hunt rats

It is always difficult to tell the Norfolk Terrier and the Norwich Terrier apart as they look virtually identical with their short, stocky bodies and their hard, wiry coats, but the easiest way to spot the difference is that the Norfolk has folding ears, which makes them look softer and, to some people, more appealing. This is a busy little terrier who is always ready for action – whether that is playing games, hiking through the woods, or chasing anything that ventures in his garden. Such an active dog needs an equally active owner who is happy to take him out in all weather and enjoy his feistiness. He is loyal and affectionate to his owner, and gets on well with well-behaved children, but is very likely to chase the neighbour's cat and shouldn't be trusted with small animals. He should be well socialised with other dogs. This is a dog that, like the Norwich, enjoys having a job to do and, with some patient training, he can excel at mini agility.

HOUSE

NORWICH TERRIER

Height	**24–25cm**
How much exercise?	🐾 🐾 🐾
How easy to train?	🐾 🐾 🐾
How noisy?	🐾 🐾 🐾
How much grooming?	🐾 🐾
How rare?	🐾 🐾 🐾 🐾 🐾

Group – Terrier
Country of origin – England
Originally bred to hunt rats

It is always difficult to tell the Norwich Terrier and the Norfolk Terrier apart as they look virtually identical with their short, stocky bodies and their hard, wiry coat, but the easiest way to spot the difference is that the Norwich has pricked ears which makes them look more alert. Like the Norfolk, this is a busy little terrier who is always ready for action, but such an active dog needs an equally active owner who is happy to take him out in all weather and enjoy his high spirits! Some people say he is slightly less on the go than the Norfolk, but it is a pretty close thing. He is loyal and affectionate to his owner, and gets on well with well-behaved children, but is very likely to chase the neighbour's cat and shouldn't be trusted with small animals. He needs plenty of socialisation with other dogs, but is more social than many terriers. His coat is easy to care for, but it does need hand stripping twice a year to remove the dead coat.

HOUSE

OLD ENGLISH SHEEPDOG

Height	56–61cm
How much exercise?	🐾 🐾 🐾 🐾
How easy to train?	🐾 🐾 🐾
How noisy?	🐾 🐾 🐾
How much grooming?	🐾 🐾 🐾 🐾 🐾
How rare?	🐾 🐾 🐾 🐾

Group – Pastoral
Country of origin – England
Originally bred for driving cattle and herding sheep

The Old English Sheepdog is one of the larger herding dogs, and has an abundant shaggy, harsh top coat with a thick undercoat. This really is a dog for people who like a lot of grooming! Like all the herding breeds, the Old English Sheepdog needs plenty of exercise if he is to stay healthy, happy and easy to live with, and so he needs a confident and active owner with plenty of time and energy to train, exercise and groom. A well-trained Old English makes a good family pet, although he is generally too big and boisterous for smaller children. They love to chase anything that moves, and may become possessive over food or toys, so careful and sensitive training is needed as this dog is just too big (and often too clumsy) to be allowed to become a canine hooligan.

HOUSE

PAPILLON

Height	20–28cm
How much exercise?	🐾 🐾 🐾
How easy to train?	🐾 🐾 🐾 🐾 🐾
How noisy?	🐾 🐾 🐾 🐾
How much grooming?	🐾 🐾 🐾 🐾
How rare?	🐾 🐾 🐾 🐾

Group – Toy
Country of origin – Belgium
Originally bred to be a companion

This dog gets his name from his large butterfly-type ears as 'papillon' is French for 'butterfly'. With his alert expression, his long, fine, silky coat, beautiful markings and trademark ears, this is a lovely looking dog who makes an ideal companion. The Papillon is not to be mistaken for a pampered lapdog though; he combines beauty and brains and can easily be trained to work at obedience, mini agility or to do tricks to entertain friends and family. This is a dog who loves to work and to learn, and owners should be prepared to put the time into training him and working with him to keep him happy and stimulated. He enjoys being with his owner and will seemingly listen to them talking for hours on end. This attachment, however, means that this is another dog who can have problems being left alone. He makes a good family dog for those with gentle children, who are prepared to take care of his long coat and who don't mind a bit of noise!

HOUSE

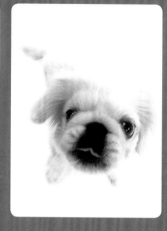

PEKINGESE

Height	15–23cm
How much exercise?	🐾
How easy to train?	🐾
How noisy?	🐾 🐾 🐾
How much grooming?	🐾 🐾 🐾 🐾
How rare?	🐾 🐾 🐾 🐾

Group – Toy
Country of Origin – China
Originally bred as a companion dog for Chinese nobility

The Pekingese is another one of those easily recognisable dogs, with his short, bowed legs, his huge, long, straight coat and thick undercoat, his impressive mane, bulbous eyes and flat face. His original breed standard was set down in the late 19th century by the Dowager Empress Tsu Hsi who stated that the breed should have "fastidious eating habits, a ruff to give him an air of dignity, hairy feet to allow him to walk silently, to have bowed legs to deter him from wandering, and to have a coat of any colour so as to suit every garment in the royal wardrobe". The Pekingese is a devoted, comical and affectionate dog to his owner, but pretty aloof to everyone else. He is stubborn and difficult to train, and his short nose and heavy coat mean that he can't walk far without tiring or overheating. He is best suited to an owner who enjoys grooming rather than long walks, and who enjoys feeling as if they are the servant to this royal canine!

HOUSE

PEMBROKE WELSH CORGI

Height	25–30cm
How much exercise?	🐾 🐾 🐾
How easy to train?	🐾 🐾
How noisy?	🐾 🐾 🐾
How much grooming?	🐾 🐾
How rare?	🐾 🐾 🐾 🐾

Group – Pastoral
Country of origin – Wales
Originally bred to drive cattle

The Pembroke Welsh Corgi is the smaller of the two Corgis, is often born without a tail, and has a medium-length straight coat with a dense undercoat to keep him warm when working. Don't let the size of this dog fool you – he is a lean mean working machine! This is a determined dog with a strong personality – let's face it, to move cows around they had to be! These dogs would drive cows by nipping at their ankles, and this trait can often still be seen in Corgis that haven't been trained otherwise! Any potential owner of a Pembroke Welsh Corgi needs to be aware that while this is a small dog, he is in no way a lapdog. This is a dog who will need plenty of exercise and training from a fairly strong-willed owner to turn him into an affectionate companion. The Pembroke Welsh Corgi can make a good family pet with training and plenty of socialisation with children – and after he is taught not to try and move children around as if they were cows!

HOUSE

POINTER

Height	**61–69cm**
How much exercise?	🐾 🐾 🐾 🐾
How easy to train?	🐾 🐾 🐾 🐾
How noisy?	🐾 🐾
How much grooming?	🐾
How rare?	🐾 🐾 🐾 🐾

Group – Gundog
Country of origin – England
Originally bred to find and indicate game

This is a fairly rarely seen, long-legged, racy-looking gundog with a gentle expression, a constantly waving tail and a fine, short coat. Like most of the gundog group, the Pointer is a kind, friendly, affectionate family dog who needs plenty of exercise and, even better, a job to do to keep him healthy and happy. This is a country dog, and is at his happiest outside with his owner tramping across the countryside, or joining in outdoor family games. He does need a lot of training though as he easily gets distracted by scents and small animals and so can become selectively deaf! He is good with other dogs, other animals and children, but he may be too boisterous for small ones. The Pointer is a perfect dog for an active, high-energy, country-living family who enjoy long walks, lots of canine games and an affectionate gentle companion.

HOUSE

POLISH LOWLAND SHEEPDOG

Height	42–50cm
How much exercise?	🐾 🐾 🐾 🐾
How easy to train?	🐾 🐾 🐾 🐾
How noisy?	🐾 🐾 🐾 🐾
How much grooming?	🐾 🐾 🐾 🐾 🐾
How rare?	🐾 🐾 🐾 🐾 🐾

Group – Pastoral
Country of origin – Poland
Originally bred for herding livestock – mostly sheep

The Polish Lowland Sheepdog is a medium sized, stocky dog with a shaggy, thick, harsh topcoat, coupled with a soft undercoat – this keeps him warm in the winter and cool in the summer. It also means that his owner needs to enjoy grooming! This fun, agile, energetic dog needs an active and fairly experienced owner to channel his boundless energy and enthusiasm in a positive way. This is an intelligent breed that learns bad habits as easily (sometimes more so!) as good ones. He can excel in any of the canine sports, and needs a job to do to stop him getting bored. By nature, he is a territorial dog who can be suspicious of strangers, and so early socialisation with people, other animals (and the postman!) is very important to make sure he lives up to his potential as an excellent, well balanced family pet. The breed is said to have a remarkable memory.

HOUSE

POMERANIAN

Height	22–28cm
How much exercise?	🐾 🐾 🐾
How easy to train?	🐾 🐾 🐾
How noisy?	🐾 🐾 🐾 🐾
How much grooming?	🐾 🐾 🐾
How rare?	🐾 🐾 🐾 🐾

Group – Toy
Country of origin – Germany
Originally bred as a companion

The Pomeranian may be the smallest of the spitz breeds, but he still has the same characteristic appearance, with his long, straight topcoat and smooth fluffy undercoat, his huge ruff, foxy face and his plumed tail held over his back. This is a busy, extrovert little dog who likes to be into everything and who enjoys exercise and games, but who can be a challenge to train as he loves to run and doesn't always come back when called! This is another small dog who is not suitable for boisterous families, both because of the risk of injury and also because a noisy family may in turn make this dog, who likes the sound of his own voice, even noisier. Despite his size, the Pomeranian makes a good watchdog – largely because he enjoys any opportunity to bark – and he will take on dogs far bigger than himself if he feels threatened. This is a good devoted companion dog for someone who has plenty of energy, doesn't mind a bit of noise and enjoys daily grooming.

HOUSE

PUG

Height	**25–28cm**
How much exercise?	🐾
How easy to train?	🐾 🐾
How noisy?	🐾 🐾
How much grooming?	🐾
How rare?	🐾 🐾

Group – Toy
Country of origin – China
Originally bred as a companion (often for royalty)

Everybody recognises the Pug as there is nothing that looks quite like him with his small compact body, his piggy tail, his bulbous eyes, his squashed nose and his short, fine coat. The Pug makes quite possibly one of the best companion dogs, as he is friendly with both owners and strangers, is playful and funny, is good with other dogs and animals and, while pocket-sized, is still robust enough to cope with family life. However, his looks tend to put some people off – although for others they are his most appealing feature. Perhaps the Pug's only drawbacks are the short hair that tends to lodge in clothing and furniture no matter how much he is groomed, and also his resistance to training as he is at heart both wilful and determined – and he snores! As they have such short noses, they can't cope with too much exercise in the summer and owners must keep the folds over his nose clean.

HOUSE

PYRENEAN MOUNTAIN DOG

Height	65–81cm
How much exercise?	🐾 🐾 🐾
How easy to train?	🐾 🐾
How noisy?	🐾 🐾 🐾 🐾
How much grooming?	🐾 🐾 🐾 🐾
How rare?	🐾 🐾 🐾 🐾 🐾

Group – Pastoral
Country of origin – France
Originally bred as a flock guard

The Pyrenean Mountain Dog is another giant of the dog world that makes a very impressive sight due to both his sheer size, and his fabulous, mostly white, long thick coat coupled with dense but fine-haired undercoat – all finished off with a stunning mane and woolly pantaloons. The breed has often been referred to as the 'animated snowdrift'. You will find his hair everywhere (even if you do the essential daily grooming); he is an expert escapologist and enthusiastic and loud guard dog; and training him to come back when called is a challenge, if not an impossibility! He will also grow into a 10-stone monster, and so if training isn't started from a very early age, you will be fighting a losing battle with a dog who may weigh more than you do! That said, with the right owner who has plenty of space, and is able to devote endless time to training, socialisation, grooming and exercise, the Pyrenean Mountain Dog makes a wonderfully loyal and loving companion.

HOUSE

RHODESIAN RIDGEBACK

Height	61–69cm
How much exercise?	🐾 🐾 🐾 🐾
How easy to train?	🐾 🐾
How noisy?	🐾
How much grooming?	🐾 🐾
How rare?	🐾 🐾

Group – Hound
Country of origin – Southern Africa
Originally bred for hunting large game (including lions)

This is an easily recognisable dog thanks to his size, his short and dense red coat, and the telltale ridge running down his back. As you can imagine from a dog who was bred to hunt lions, this is a powerful, strong-willed, confident dog who needs an experienced, active owner to ensure he gets the training, exercise and socialisation he needs. The Rhodesian Ridgeback is also a somewhat aloof and independent breed, and training will be a bit of a challenge as he will often ignore a request unless he sees a good reason for it! He can also be difficult to control on the lead, and can easily take his owner grass-skiing! The Rhodesian Ridgeback loves to chase – and so he may not be safe with the cat or any small animals – but he is good with older children. With an experienced owner, this formidable and stunning-looking dog can be a joy to own, and while an active, alert hunter outside, he can be a real couch potato in the house.

HOUSE

ROTTWEILER

Height	**58–69cm**
How much exercise?	🐾 🐾 🐾 🐾
How easy to train?	🐾 🐾 🐾
How noisy?	🐾 🐾 🐾
How much grooming?	🐾 🐾
How rare?	🐾

Group – Working
Country of origin – Germany
Originally bred as a cattle herder

Everybody recognises the Rottweiler, even if it is just so they can cross the road to avoid a dog with such a fearsome, and largely undeserved, reputation. His looks don't help, however, as he looks a bit like a nightclub bouncer with his swaggering walk, his broad head, his compact and powerful body and his short, thick, glossy black and tan coat. The Rottweiler is a powerful, active working dog and as such he needs an experienced, firm but fair, owner to make sure he gets all the socialisation and training he needs to be a safe and friendly member of society. Having said that, a well-trained and well-loved Rottweiler is no more and no less dangerous than any other large powerful dog, but somehow, due to irresponsible owners who want them as status symbols, they get a lot of bad press. Their short coat makes takes little grooming, but the amount of work needed to keep them mentally and physically stimulated, and adequately socialised, makes them high-maintenance dogs for expert owners only.

HOUSE

ROUGH COLLIE

Height	51–61cm
How much exercise?	🐾 🐾 🐾 🐾
How easy to train?	🐾 🐾 🐾 🐾
How noisy?	🐾 🐾 🐾
How much grooming?	🐾 🐾 🐾 🐾 🐾
How rare?	🐾 🐾 🐾

Group – Pastoral
Country of origin – Scotland
Originally bred for herding sheep

The Rough Collie is probably one of the most well-known and easily recognised of the herding breeds with film star looks, long nose, heavy thick coat with a soft furry undercoat and often with an almost lion-like mane. This is another breed that needs a lot of grooming to keep him healthy and happy, and also a lot of socialisation to overcome his sensitive and rather reserved nature towards anything new, other dogs and strangers. They do, however, form a very strong bond with their owners and will do anything they can to try and please them, and so can excel at training and obedience. These dogs need sensitive, grooming-loving owners who are looking for a very close bond with their dog, and who will spend time with them to help them get over their natural shyness and discover the exceptional dog lurking within.

HOUSE

SALUKI

Height	58–71cm
How much exercise?	🐾 🐾 🐾 🐾 🐾
How easy to train?	🐾
How noisy?	🐾 🐾
How much grooming?	🐾 🐾
How rare?	🐾 🐾 🐾 🐾 🐾

Group – Hound
Country of origin – Middle East
Originally bred to hunt hares, foxes and gazelles

The Saluki is one of the most ancient of dog breeds, and has had the most royal of pasts. As such he looks every inch the aristocrat with the lean, streamlined body-shape common to all the sight hounds, covered with a soft, silky coat, but coupled with elegant feathering of his ears and tail. This is a dog who seems to remember his regal past, and seems to feel that training and in fact listening to any commands at all is totally beneath him. His passion is to run and chase, and he will be totally deaf to any attempts to stop him. This means that owners need plenty of secure space to allow him to run safely. This is a breed that seems to appeal to cat lovers, as they are used to their animals being somewhat superior and independent. The Saluki is independent minded and needs an owner who can appreciate this elegant, sensitive and gentle dog without expecting fawning affection in return.

HOUSE

SAMOYED

Height	**46–56cm**
How much exercise?	🐾 🐾 🐾 ½
How easy to train?	🐾 🐾
How noisy?	🐾 🐾 🐾 🐾 ½
How much grooming?	🐾 🐾 🐾 🐾 🐾
How rare?	🐾 🐾 🐾 🐾 🐾

Group – Pastoral
Country of origin – Russia
Originally bred for herding reindeer

The Samoyed is a fabulous dog to look at, and once seen they are never forgotten. They have traffic-stopping good looks with their cloud of thick, white, soft hair with short, dense undercoat, luxurious mane, tightly curled tail and teddy bear ears. The Samoyed is a happy dog who loves everyone. Owners need to love grooming as this is a dog that takes plenty of brushing to keep his coat healthy and looking its best, and to prevent the house being constantly covered in hair. As could be expected of a breed used to pull sledges, the Samoyed is inclined to pull on the lead and is amazingly strong. This is a cheerful, active, alert dog whose stubbornness often masks his intelligence. He needs an owner who is prepared to train him, to keep him under control (but doesn't expect an obedience champion!), isn't too house-proud, and who likes to live in colder climates, as he overheats easily and so tropical central heating will make him miserable.

SCOTTISH TERRIER

Height	**25–28cm**
How much exercise?	🐾 🐾 🐾
How easy to train?	🐾 🐾
How noisy?	🐾 🐾 🐾 🐾
How much grooming?	🐾 🐾 🐾
How rare?	🐾 🐾 🐾

Group – Terrier
Country of origin – Scotland
Originally bred to kill any vermin

While this is a dog that isn't seen anywhere near as often as his white West Highland cousin, he is just as distinctive with his bushy eyebrows, thick beard, pricked ears and wiry, harsh, often black topcoat. The Scottish Terrier is terrier through and through: stubborn and wilful, often feisty and is a challenge to train. However, with owners that he respects, he is intensely loyal and affectionate, and when trained (which can be a challenge), he is a fabulous dog to live with. He will get on with well-trained children, but possibly not the cat! The Scottie has a strong personality and is full of character, and so needs an active owner who is determined, firm and fair, and who can give him the exercise, training and socialisation he needs to be the exceptional dog that he can be. The Scottish Terrier doesn't need too much grooming, but does need hand-stripping twice a year to get rid of the dead coat.

HOUSE

SHAR PEI

Height	46–51cm
How much exercise?	🐾 🐾 🐾
How easy to train?	🐾
How noisy?	🐾
How much grooming?	🐾 🐾
How rare?	🐾 🐾

Group – Utility
Country of origin – China
Originally bred as a fighting dog

There is nothing that looks anything like the Shar Pei. This is a dog whose skin seems several sizes too big for him – especially when he is a puppy – and by the time you couple this with his short prickly coat, his blue tongue, and his high-set round tail, he really does look utterly unique. The Shar Pei is a tricky dog to own. He is prone to skin and eye problems because of his deep folds of skin, he has a tendency to be aggressive to other dogs, and he is stubborn, headstrong and aloof, thinking that training is totally beneath him! He needs a firm, experienced and confident owner who has plenty of time to socialise him with both people and other dogs. He is, therefore, not an ideal family pet and is better suited to an expert with experience of this unique and fascinating breed. His prickly coat tends to lodge itself in clothing and furniture, and he needs his skin folds cleaning daily to prevent infections.

SHETLAND SHEEPDOG

Height	36–37cm
How much exercise?	🐾 🐾 🐾
How easy to train?	🐾 🐾 🐾 🐾 🐾
How noisy?	🐾 🐾 🐾 🐾
How much grooming?	🐾 🐾 🐾 🐾
How rare?	🐾 🐾

Group – Pastoral
Country of origin – Shetland Isles, Scotland
Originally bred for herding sheep

The Shetland Sheepdog is a perfect miniature of his larger, film star cousin, the Rough Collie. He has exactly the same long nose, alert expression, flamboyant mane and long, harsh, straight topcoat, with soft, dense undercoat. While the Shetland Sheepdog may look like a pocket sized Lassie, owners mustn't forget that at heart he is every bit a working dog. The Sheltie is a delight to train, excels in obedience, agility or flyball, and will even herd sheep if given the chance. Shetland Sheepdogs bond very closely to their owners and are affectionate, devoted and responsive to them. However, with strangers they can be reserved, quiet and almost timid and so need plenty of socialisation, to prevent excessive shyness, and a fairly quiet household. This is not a dog for boisterous families. The Shetland Sheepdog also needs an owner who enjoys grooming as his thick coat can easily tangle.

HOUSE

SHIBA INU

Height	36.5–39.5cm
How much exercise?	🐾 🐾 🐾
How easy to train?	🐾
How noisy?	🐾 🐾
How much grooming?	🐾 🐾
How rare?	🐾 🐾 🐾 🐾 🐾

Group – Utility
Country of origin – Japan
Originally bred to hunt small game

The Shiba Inu is a spitz-type dog and has a very distinctive, almost fox-like, look with his thick curved tail and his intense red coat that couples a hard, straight topcoat with a soft, dense undercoat. He does come in other colours, but the red is still the most popular. While the Shiba Inu isn't a big dog, he is still quite a challenge. He is bold, spirited and almost cat-like, and while he is the most adorable cute fluff-ball puppy, he soon grows into a strong and independent dog who is resistant to training. Despite their thick coats, these dogs don't need much grooming (except when shedding) as they are a very clean breed – another way in which they are like cats. They are affectionate with their owners but are not cuddly or emotional dogs. The Shiba Inu needs a confident, experienced owner who has plenty of time to both train and socialise this strong-willed dog, and understand his fascinating personality.

HOUSE

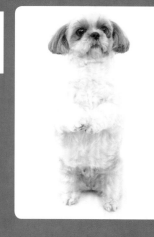

SHIH TZU

Height	25–27cm
How much exercise?	🐾 🐾
How easy to train?	🐾 🐾 🐾
How noisy?	🐾 🐾 🐾
How much grooming?	🐾 🐾 🐾 🐾
How rare?	🐾

Group – Utility
Country of origin – China
Originally bred as a companion dog

The Shih Tzu is an excellent choice for a companion dog although his long dense topcoat and extensive undercoat mean that potential owners must like grooming – unless they plan to keep him clipped! This is a happy, friendly dog who loves life and is equally at home tramping across the countryside as he is cuddling up as a lapdog. The Shih Tzu is active and alert, and will enjoy playing with all members of the family. He is certainly clever enough to be trained to do everything from basic obedience to clever tricks, which he will enjoy showing off! The Shih Tzu loves company and may suffer from separation anxiety when left alone. This is a dog who loves everyone, and if well socialised he will get on with other dogs and any other animals he finds himself living with.

HOUSE

SIBERIAN HUSKY

Height	51–60cm
How much exercise?	🐾 🐾 🐾 🐾 🐾 🐾
How easy to train?	🐾 🐾
How noisy?	🐾 🐾 🐾 🐾
How much grooming?	🐾 🐾 🐾 🐾
How rare?	🐾 🐾

Group – Working
Country of origin – Russia
Originally bred as a sled dog

The Siberian Husky is a truly stunning dog with more than a passing resemblance to the wolf with his erect ears, long nose and his thick coat and dense undercoat to protect him from extremes of temperature down to an unimaginable –60˚C. This is without doubt a dog for the enthusiast only, as he was born to run and so needs endless exercise, but is unlikely ever to be reliable off the lead. As such, owners need to find a way to keep him healthy and happy, and this may mean running or cycling several miles a day with him, or maybe even finding a way to harness his natural sled-pulling ability. Some owners work their dogs with land sleds on forest tracks, while other Siberian Huskies excel pulling skiers using specially adapted harnesses in a new sport called ski-pulka. This is a friendly dog bred to live as a pack, and so he needs plenty of company – canine or human. Owners also have to enjoy grooming and not mind hair as he sheds almost constantly.

HOUSE

SPRINGER SPANIEL

Height	46–52cm
How much exercise?	🐾 🐾 🐾 🐾 🐾
How easy to train?	🐾 🐾 🐾 🐾
How noisy?	🐾 🐾
How much grooming?	🐾 🐾 🐾
How rare?	🐾

Group – Gundog
Country of origin – England
Originally bred for flushing game

This happy, friendly, enthusiastic member of the Spaniel family can easily be recognised by his size (he is larger then the Cocker) but with similar long, curly ears and medium-length feathered coat. The Springer Spaniel is a high-energy dog who needs active owners and endless exercise to keep him happy. Providing he is kept stimulated and well exercised he makes an excellent family pet, as he loves everyone he meets – even, with some training, the cat! As he is at heart a country dog, he will need daily grooming, as he will bring a lot of the great outdoors back indoors. This is a dog who will enjoy training, and can excel in any of the canine sports, especially agility, if you can motivate him and keep his attention. This is a real family dog – as long as the family is active!

HOUSE

STANDARD POODLE

Height	**over 38cm**
How much exercise?	🐾 🐾 🐾 🐾
How easy to train?	🐾 🐾 🐾 🐾
How noisy?	🐾 🐾
How much grooming?	🐾 🐾 🐾 🐾 🐾
How rare?	🐾 🐾 🐾 🐾

Group – Utility
Country of origin – Germany
Originally bred as a water retrieving dog

There is nothing as distinctive as a Standard Poodle, and no matter what kind of hairdo he may be sporting, he is easily recognised with his long pointy nose, his flamboyant attitude and his profuse, dense, non-shedding wavy coat. While the Standard Poodle may look somewhat like a supermodel, they are actually workers at heart, and are active, happy dogs full of energy and fun. They are easy to train, devoted to their owner, love children (although can knock over small ones) and will even get on with the cat. In fact, this dog loves everyone! He does need lots of exercise, though, so he doesn't do well with couch potato owners. Many Standard Poodle owners find that they can compete very successfully in agility or obedience, and that these lively dogs thrive with a job to do. Owners of Poodles have to enjoy grooming or be prepared to pay a professional. Their coat doesn't shed and so needs clipping or trimming every couple of months.

HOUSE

ST BERNARD

Height	over 70cm
How much exercise?	🐾 🐾
How easy to train?	🐾 🐾
How noisy?	🐾 🐾
How much grooming?	🐾 🐾 🐾 🐾
How rare?	🐾 🐾 🐾 🐾

Group – Working
Country of origin – Switzerland
Originally bred as a rescue dog

The St Bernard is a true giant of the dog world, and everybody recognises this legendary life-saving dog with his massive jowled head, gentle eyes, and short, thick, orange and white coat. This is a dog that needs a huge house to live in, and one that isn't too hot. The St Bernard is a challenge to train, and needs to be handled with kind understanding and not force – mostly because you can't force a dog that size to do anything! Having said that, he is a kind, affectionate companion who takes life pretty much as it comes. They are loyal to their owners and families, and some (especially males) can be protective and territorial so they need plenty of socialisation when they are young to overcome this before they become too big to manage. With the right owner, socialising, training, and plenty of space, the St Bernard makes a good companion who is happy to join in with everything from pulling a cart to just hanging out.

HOUSE

STAFFORDSHIRE BULL TERRIER

Height	36–41cm
How much exercise?	🐾 🐾 🐾
How easy to train?	🐾 🐾 🐾
How noisy?	🐾 🐾
How much grooming?	🐾
How rare?	🐾

Group – Terrier
Country of Origin – England
Originally bred for dog fighting

Everybody recognises the Staffordshire Bull Terrier with his short, smooth coat, his stocky body and his huge grin, and he is the most popular of all the terriers in the UK. The Staffordshire Bull Terrier has had very bad press due to irresponsible dog owners who do not realise the amount of socialisation and training this strong and powerful breed needs to ensure he is friendly and reliable with other dogs. As a family dog he is truly excellent and is utterly devoted and friendly to all the family, although he may be too boisterous and playful for small children, and their games can get too exciting for him. This is also a dog who may never be safe with cats or small animals. The Staffordshire Bull Terrier does everything at full-throttle – including play, exercise and love – this is a full-on dog! This is a dog for an active, affectionate, experienced, responsible owner who is prepared to put a lot of time into his training and socialisation.

HOUSE

TIBETAN SPANIEL

Height	24–25cm
How much exercise?	🐾 🐾
How easy to train?	🐾 🐾
How noisy?	🐾 🐾 🐾 🐾
How much grooming?	🐾 🐾 🐾
How rare?	🐾 🐾 🐾 🐾 🐾

Group – Utility
Country of origin – Tibet
Originally bred as a companion/monastery watchdog

The Tibetan Spaniel doesn't look much like any of the working spaniels we are used to. Instead he is a smallish dog and has a short nose, silky mane, curled and plumed tail, tiny feet and small body covered in a long silky topcoat and fine but thick undercoat. This breed make good pets, being friendly, playful and robust enough to cope with the whole family (as long as they aren't too boisterous). However, they do tend to be rather independent and, on occasion, somewhat aloof, making training and motivating them a challenge. The Tibetan Spaniel is an alert, curious breed who enjoys games and exercise, but is equally happy to be a lapdog (as long as he gets an outlet for his spurts of energy). He needs an owner who enjoys daily grooming and walks, and who doesn't mind a bit of noise!

HOUSE

WEIMARANER

Height	**56–69cm**
How much exercise?	🐾 🐾 🐾 🐾 🐾 🐾
How easy to train?	🐾 🐾 🐾
How noisy?	🐾 🐾 🐾
How much grooming?	🐾
How rare?	🐾 🐾

Group – Gundog
Country of origin – Germany
Originally bred to point (indicate) game

The Weimaraner is a distinctive-looking dog who certainly lives up to his nickname, the 'Grey Ghost', with his tall, elegant looks and his short silver-grey almost phantom-like, shimmering metallic coat. This is an energetic, highly active dog that needs plenty of exercise to keep him healthy and happy. Without it, he can become destructive, boisterous, or Houdini-esque! He needs lots of socialisation to ensure he gets on with other dogs, but apart from that he is friendly with everyone, although probably just too bouncy for smaller children, and some just can't stand cats! The Weimaraner can be a challenge to train as he is often stubborn and strong willed, and he needs an experienced owner to get the best out of him. Once convinced to work, the Weimaraner loves to be challenged by training, and for many agility is an ideal answer. This is a tactile, affectionate dog who will be devoted to his owner, but will never be blindly obedient!

HOUSE

WELSH TERRIER

Height	36–39cm
How much exercise?	🐾 🐾 🐾
How easy to train?	🐾 🐾 🐾
How noisy?	🐾 🐾 🐾 🐾
How much grooming?	🐾 🐾 🐾
How rare?	🐾 🐾 🐾 🐾 🐾

Group – Terrier
Country of origin – Wales
Originally bred to hunt native mammals

The Welsh Terrier is similar in appearance to a small Airedale with similar colour and markings, beard and wiry, hard, thick coat. This is another terrier who is always busy and on the go. He is active, alert and curious – and into everything! The Welsh Terrier is still full of the old hunting spirit and so will enjoy games that involve hunting, chasing (and often destroying!) toys. He is a challenge to train, but once he respects his owner, he is unswervingly loyal, affectionate and eager to please. Like most terriers, he will get on with sensible, older children, but possibly not with the cat. Other small animals are definite no-nos! He needs plenty of socialisation to make sure he gets on with other dogs. This is a dog with a nose for mischief and so owners will need a sense of humour – and a well-fenced garden! Grooming is fairly minimal, but he does need regular hand stripping and trimming to keep his coat healthy and tidy.

HOUSE

WEST HIGHLAND WHITE TERRIER

Height	**28cm**
How much exercise?	🐾 🐾 🐾
How easy to train?	🐾 🐾 🐾
How noisy?	🐾 🐾 🐾 🐾 🐾
How much grooming?	🐾 🐾 🐾
How rare?	🐾

Group – Terrier
Country of origin – Scotland
Originally bred to hunt and kill rats and other vermin

The West Highland White Terrier may be small, but is a real giant when it comes to personality. This is one of the most popular breeds in the UK, and with his distinctive white coat, which is harsh on top but with a soft undercoat, is probably one of the most easily recognised and frequently seen breeds. This is an active, alert, courageous, fun and often feisty little dog who should never be considered a lapdog. He needs a fairly strong-willed owner and lots of exercise and training to turn him into an ideal companion. While this is a friendly breed, like most terriers he may not be reliable with cats and other small animals. A well-trained Westie can certainly excel in mini agility, which will help to burn off energy. The Westie is a notoriously noisy breed, and while with good training and lots of stimulation this can be reduced, potential owners are going to have to want a dog who likes the sound of his own voice!

HOUSE

WIRE FOX TERRIER

Height	38.5–39.5cm
How much exercise?	🐾 🐾 🐾 🐾
How easy to train?	🐾 🐾
How noisy?	🐾 🐾 🐾 🐾 🐾
How much grooming?	🐾 🐾 🐾
How rare?	🐾 🐾 🐾 🐾

Group – Terrier
Country of origin – England
Originally bred for hunting foxes

The Wire Fox Terrier is a very smart looking dog, and is easily recognised with his long nose, beard, and mostly white, very wiry coat. At heart, the Fox Terrier is still a working dog, and he loves nothing more than a chance to chase, hunt, rip and tear, so owners need to find games and toys to satisfy that urge. With an owner he respects, he is a loyal, affectionate dog, and he gets on well with sensible children – the cat and other small hairies are a very different matter, however! He is a challenge to train, as he is just too active to listen – and often too independent to care – but despite that, he is an enchanting dog for active owners with a sense of humour. For owners with the patience to train and socialise him, he can compete in the canine sports such as agility with ease – as everything is done at top speed! The Wire Fox Terrier doesn't need too much grooming, but he does need hand stripping to keep his coat healthy and tidy.

HOUSE

YORKSHIRE TERRIER

Height	22.5–23.5cm
How much exercise?	🐾 🐾 🐾 🐾
How easy to train?	🐾 🐾 🐾
How noisy?	🐾 🐾 🐾 🐾 🐾
How much grooming?	🐾 🐾 🐾 🐾
How rare?	🐾

Group – Terrier
Country of origin – England
Originally bred to kill rats in mines

The Yorkshire Terrier is one of the easiest of the terriers to recognise by his diminutive size and his long, shiny, silky blue and tan coat. Even when clipped, his striking colour always gives him away. Despite his size, the Yorkshire Terrier is still very much a working dog and is on the go all the time. This is a huge dog in a small body! He is lively and curious and into everything, and owners will have to get used to being tailed everywhere by their inquisitive (and often noisy) shadow. This is a dog who needs lots of exercise and stimulation – he loves long walks, but also needs games in the house to keep his busy mind occupied. The Yorkshire Terrier is one of the more trainable terriers, but even then, sometimes the thrill of the chase is too strong. He is affectionate and loyal to his owners, can get on with sensible children and can learn to live with his own cats, but the neighbour's cat should beware!

HOUSE

TOP 5 DOGS FOR FIRST TIME OWNERS

These dogs are ideal for owners who have never had a dog before and want to start off with one who will be easy to own, simple to train and fun to have in their life. These breeds provide a gentle (although in some cases still active) introduction to dog ownership.

Cavalier King Charles Spaniel

2 Labrador Retriever

3 Flat coated Retriever

4 Pug

5 Poodle – all sizes

TOP 5 DOGS WITH CHILDREN

These are dogs who will get on well with children and will happily join in with family life. Many of these are from the gundog group as this group is full of happy, easy-going, soft-mouthed dogs. However, all dogs and children who are going to live together must be well trained!

Labrador Retriever

Golden Retriever

Springer Spaniel

Beagle

Irish Setter

TOP 5 DOGS FOR FITNESS FANATICS

Some dogs need almost endless exercise and are only happy when either tramping across the countryside, or else home exhausted after another day of constant activity. These are dogs for the seriously active only!

Border Collie

Siberian Husky

Dalmatian

Weimaraner

Springer Spaniel

TOP 5 DOGS FOR COUCH POTATOES

While some dogs enjoy endless exercise, some are far happier lying at their owner's feet, on their knee or upside down on the sofa for hours on end. Their idea of exercise is walking to their food bowl. While they still need a daily walk, and can manage short bursts of energy, these are the real layabouts of the dog world. And some snore!

Bulldog

HOUSE

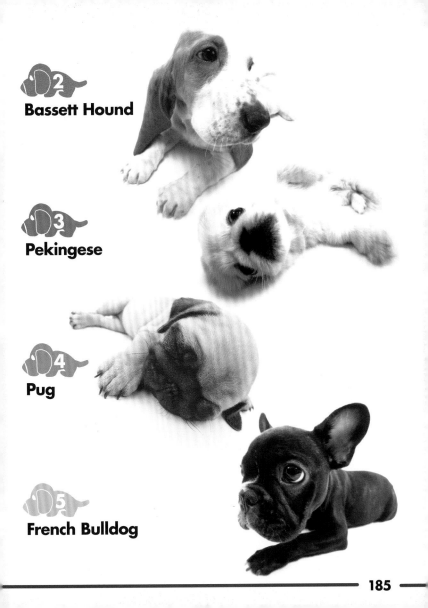

2 Bassett Hound

3 Pekingese

4 Pug

5 French Bulldog

TOP 5 DOGS FOR GROOMING LOVERS

While some dogs can look clean and smart with just a weekly wipe over, these dogs need daily brushing, right down to the skin (which can be a long way down and take a long time!) to keep them healthy, tangle-free and looking good and/or to stop them shedding endless hair on the furniture!

Old English Sheepdog

Samoyed

Polish Lowland Sheepdog

Bearded Collie

Siberian Husky

TOP 5 DOGS FOR EXPERTS ONLY

While there are dogs ideal for first-time owners, these dogs, fabulous though they are, are definitely more demanding, and, to make good companions, are strictly for experienced owners only.

Akita

2 Bouvier des Flaunders

3 Chow Chow

4 Rottweiler

5 Shiba Inu

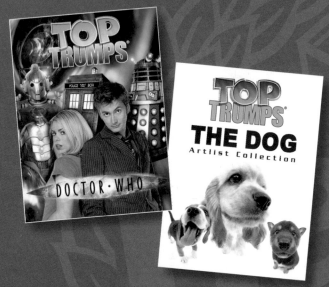